João Batista Mulato Santos

...igion in Ludwig Feuerbach

João Batista Mulato Santos

The Fundamental Principle of Religion in Ludwig Feuerbach

The Awakening of the Religious Feeling

ScienciaScripts

Imprint

Any brand names and product names mentioned in this book are subject to trademark, brand or patent protection and are trademarks or registered trademarks of their respective holders. The use of brand names, product names, common names, trade names, product descriptions etc. even without a particular marking in this work is in no way to be construed to mean that such names may be regarded as unrestricted in respect of trademark and brand protection legislation and could thus be used by anyone.

Cover image: www.ingimage.com

This book is a translation from the original published under ISBN 978-620-2-40973-5.

Publisher:
Sciencia Scripts
is a trademark of
Dodo Books Indian Ocean Ltd. and OmniScriptum S.R.L publishing group

120 High Road, East Finchley, London, N2 9ED, United Kingdom
Str. Armeneasca 28/1, office 1, Chisinau MD-2012, Republic of Moldova, Europe

ISBN: 978-620-8-34633-1

Copyright © João Batista Mulato Santos
Copyright © 2024 Dodo Books Indian Ocean Ltd. and OmniScriptum S.R.L publishing group

*To my friends and family.
In particular, to my mother Maria da Conceiqao Damiao
Santos, my sister and my father Joao Mulato dos Santos, for
their trust, love and unconditional support at all times.*

In no way am I saying that God is nothing, that the Trinity is nothing, that the Word of God is nothing, etc. That would be too easy! I only show that these symbols are not what their theology makes them out to be.

INDICE

Chapter 1   8

Chapter 2   33

Chapter 3   47

INTRODUCTION

This work, the result of a year and a half of monographic research, aims to find the determining element in the foundation of religion, present in the materialist philosophy of the German philosopher Ludwig Andreas Feuerbach (1804-1872). To this end, his main works *The Essence of Christianity* (1841) and *Preleoges on the Essence of Religion* (1851) will be analyzed. In the two works used in this study, the different perspectives presented by Feuerbach on the same theme will be confronted. At first, in *The Essence of Christianity*, the author bases religious sentiment from an anthropological point of view, in which he describes man, as a generic being, as the bearer of a whole perfection that is only possible for the human race and not for the human individual.

The other analysis that follows, made from a psychological perspective, shows how the impressions that come from nature engrave in man the elements that allow the gods to appear in his life, according to *Prelegoes on the Essence of Religion*. So we have an impasse between the two arguments that support the existence of religion. On the one hand, it is the generic essence of man, objectified in God, that presents itself as the primary foundation for religion, while on the other, the non-reciprocal relationship between man and nature causes gods to emerge in man's life, the main foundations being a sense of dependence and egoism. It is therefore necessary to find what is the basic foundation, the most appropriate explanation of religious sentiment, through the two works mentioned above.

Ludwig Andreas Feuerbach was born on July 28, 1804 in Landshut, Bavaria, Germany, and died on September 13, 1872 in Rechenberg, Nuremberg, Germany. He was the son of a prominent jurist and became a seminarian at a young age. However, he abandoned his studies in theology to devote himself to philosophy, as he himself said in a letter to his brother in 1825: "I have exchanged theology for philosophy. Outside philosophy there is no salvation." (REDYSON. 2011, p. 08.) and went to Berlin where he became a student of the then famous philosopher Georg Wilhelm Friedrich Hegel (1770-1831).

Feuerbach was initially a staunch Hegelian, part of the German Idealism philosophical movement, but over time, with his studies and theoretical development, he made a transition to the scientific materialism of the second half of the 19th century. His thinking contrasts with that of the great philosophers of modern times such as Descartes, Spinoza, Leibniz and even Kant. However, his philosophy undoubtedly ran counter to that of his former teacher, Hegel. He became an energetic fighter against the philosophical current of his master, about which he claimed that in order to understand it, we should study it in reverse, because Hegel's speculative philosophy described man upside down.

Feuerbach's influence on Hegel is remarkable, as is his influence on Marx. For many, Feuerbach is just a philosopher who finds himself between Hegelian and Marxist thought, but by dealing with the theme of religion in his books in an absolutely serene way and focusing on human dramas, the philosopher ended up entering the history of the philosophy of religion as one of the main names. He even served as the basis for psychoanalysis, since Freud's interpretation of dream symbols in his psychoanalytic method is similar to what Feuerbach does with the sacred symbols of faith, which for some can be understood as the outlines of a psychology based on the dreams of Christianity.

In his works, Feuerbach makes it clear that religion, for him, is not a silly and empty subject, but a means by which man tries to express exactly all his dreams and desires. In this sense, this research tries to elucidate a problematic between two of his main works, *The Essence of Christianity* (1841) and *Prelegoes on the Essence of Religion* (1851), regarding the fundamental principle of the essence of religion, that is, what actually makes man believe in the mystical, the supernatural, in religion? What makes the gods appear in human life.

Starting with Chapter 1: *The Foundations of Religion*, this research focuses on firstly exposing the problematic between *The Essence of Christianity* and Lectures *on the Essence of Religion*. This initial chapter aims to demonstrate the rationale that Feuerbach uses in both works and the divergent perspectives when dealing with the same theme, namely the fundamental principle of religion. In this sense, subchapter 1.1 *The Foundation of Religion in The Essence of Christianity* analyzes the importance and the methods that the philosopher uses to understand religion until he arrives at the generic essence of man. In addressing the essence of the human race, Feuerbach bases religion on man himself, stating that God is nothing more than the human essence objectified and projected onto an entity that actually refers to man, since it coincides with him. In subchapter 1.2 *The Basis of Religion in the Lectures on the Essence of Religion,* the argument changes its perspective a little and focuses on the psychological explanation for the religious phenomenon, finding in the relationship between man and nature the necessary basis for the essence of religion. The feeling of dependence stands out as an important element in understanding religious sentiment. However, a more complete approach to this concept will only be made in the third chapter, when the question of egoism will also be included. Finally, subchapter 1.3 *The Foundations of Religion in Feuerbach* will question the existing problematics and the possible conclusions that can be reached.

In Chapter 2: *The Generic Essence of Man,* an analysis is made of the book *The Essence of Christianity*, making clear the anthropological perspective that Feuerbach uses to base religion, starting with the concept of man in the first subchapter under the title *2.1 Man in Feuerbach*. This explains the differences between man in the individual sense and man in the general sense, so that we can understand the perfection that exists in the human race. Subchapter *2.2 Consciousness* deals with the theme that leads man to the condition of a specific being capable of having his own genus as an object of knowledge. Subchapter 2.3 *The Theory of Objectification* explains the importance of objects in man's life. Feuerbach states that man only comes into contact with his essence through objects, and so God appears as a spiritual object through which man's generic essence is revealed.

The last chapter, *3: The Subjective Foundation of Religion*, as the title suggests, will be dedicated to the subjective aspect of religion that Feuerbach exposes throughout his lectures of 1851. In this section, the feeling of dependence and all the others that stem from it are highlighted, as is fear, which is shown to be extremely necessary for the emergence of religion, as is egoism. The subchapters are *3.1 The Feeling of Dependence and Fear, 3.2 Egoism* and the conclusion is in the last subchapter, 3.3 *The Anthropological and Subjective Foundations of Religion,* where a reconciliation will be made between the two works in order to clarify what the fundamental principle of religion is based on the two approaches taken by the philosopher.

CHAPTER I: THE FOUNDATION OF RELIGION

1.1 The Foundations of Religion in *The Essence of Christianity*

In Feuerbach's philosophy there is always a recurring theme that is explored countless times in his various publications: the religious question. Religion has always been, and still is, a very delicate and polemical subject to deal with, which is why it has often been avoided or exposed in a moderate and partial way by most authors. Even Kant, who, after the unfavorable criticism of his *Critique of Pure Reason* (1781), knowingly wrote in the preface to the second edition that he preferred faith in God to giving space to knowledge.

Feuerbach went further, dared like no other and managed to discover what the codes of religious sentiment are and laid them out throughout his main works, which are studied in this research. These are *The Essence of Christianity,* published in 1841, and *Lectures on the Essence of* Religion, written in 1848 but not published until 1851, which were written at the request of students at the Heidelberg university where he worked. It is important to remember that both works were published in 19th century Germany, which was going through serious political and religious conflicts and became the subject of immense repercussions, which led to the author's departure from his academic career. He began to live in isolation in the countryside, and in this way, according to him, he unlearned the art of speech by assuming his thoughts with extreme conviction:

> Feuerbach was punished as an arsonist. Those who read him were burned, and for this he suffered the punishment of intellectual exile for the rest of his life. So much so that, when he delivered these *Lectures on the Essence of Religion*, he apologized to his listeners, saying that he had unlearned the art of speech. He therefore belongs to what was characteristic of the Protestant spirit - which has almost disappeared today - which is the courage to take on the convictions of feeling and

reason at any price, even in complete solitude .[1]

In *The Essence of Christianity* (1841), Feuerbach aims to reveal the secrets of the essence of the Christian religion covered by the cloak of the supernatural and, from then on, to decode the sacred symbols of Christianity, showing that what religion expresses as something beyond refers to something below, without at any time failing to give the due importance that religious matters deserve. His philosophy focuses on developing a "human model of reason", as Adriana Serrao points out, but also on guiding man towards a reunion with himself, or rather, with his own essence.

> (...) Feuerbach's thought is mobilized by a central intuition, which must even be considered as its unique problem: the simultaneous establishment of *a human model of reason* and an integral conception of the human being .[2]

To this end, the author uses various historical devices to explain and provide a philosophical foundation for how the Christian religion truly expresses the human essence. This procedure he calls historico-philosophical because it goes beyond a mere concern with the veracity of the supernatural events reported in religious books and focuses on understanding the reasons that led men to record such events as fantastical events and what they mean from a more reflective, philosophical point of view.

> (...) my book is nothing more than a faithful analysis, which sticks to its object in the most rigorous way, a historical and philosophical analysis, the "self-disillusionment", the "self-consciousness" of religion. A historical-philosophical analysis, in contrast to the purely historical analyses of Christianity. The historian shows, like Daumer for example, that the supper is a ritual originating from ancient human sacrifice, that in ancient times, instead of bread and wine, real human flesh and blood was digested. I, however, take as the object of my analysis

---

[1] FEUERBACH. Ludwig. [1851]. *Lectures on the Essence of Religion.* Trad. By Jose da Silva Brandao. Papirus editora. 1989, p.07.
[2] SERRAO, Adriana Verissimo [1999]. *The Humanity of Reason - Ludwig Feuerbach and the Project of an Integral Anthropology.* Lisbon: Calouste Gulbenkian Foundation, p. 20.

> and reduction only the Christian meaning of it or the meaning sanctioned by Christianity and I follow the principle that only the meaning that a dogma or institution has for Christianity (...). I don't ask whether this or that, but whether the miracle in general can happen or not; I only show what the miracle is and not *a priori*, but through the examples of miracles that are narrated in the Bible as real facts and with this I solve exactly the question of the possibility, reality or necessity of the miracle in a way that annuls even the possibility of these questions.[3]

In *The Essence of Christianity*, Feuerbach sets out to expose the fundamental elements that underpin the Christian religion, in a detailed and precise way, as only someone who is passionate about the subject could do. In this work he details the main points for understanding what Christianity is based on, without considering any abstract principles, but at no point does he try to simply destroy it or silence its voice by sentencing it as a mere illusion or a chimera, something already done by other philosophers.

> (...) I don't say absolutely (and how easy that would be for me!) - God is nothing, the Trinity is nothing, the word of God is nothing, etc, I only show that such things are not what they are in the illusion of theology, that they are not strange but intimate mysteries, the mysteries of human nature; I only show that religion takes the apparent and superficial essence of nature and humanity for its true and inner essence and therefore imagines the true esoteric essence of it as a strange and special essence (...).[4]

But, contrary to this, the atheist philosopher wants to rediscover it and, in this way, also rediscover man. By understanding Christian religion, we can better understand Christian man, because religion expresses what man is, what he desires, his greatest longings, loves, fears and highest and deepest feelings, since theology is, for Feuerbach, the same as anthropology.

In his quest to understand Christian man and, consequently, Christian

---

[3] FEUERBACH, Ludwig. *The Essence of Christianity*. [1841]. Trad. By Jose da Silva Brandao. Papirus editora. 2007, p. 26-27.
[4] FEUERBACH, Ludwig. *The Essence of Christianity*. [1841]. Trad. By Jose da Silva Brandao. Papirus editora. 2007, p. 24.

religion, Feuerbach comes across a type of religious man that is different from the rest. The Christian detaches himself from the peculiarities of his species, i.e. the beliefs that only make sense to a certain people, and elevates himself to universal pretensions, since his God makes sense to any human being. Regardless of nationality or ethnicity, anyone can become a Christian without any great demands. Christianity therefore reaches everyone, because it is based on what each and every individual possesses, that is, an essence.

The generic essence of man is what is most intimate, defines and grounds him. This essence is made up of three elements common to all, that is, they are essences that define what a man is in his entirety. Will, reason and heart are absolute and perfect elements because they are ends in themselves. In this sense:

> A complete man possesses strength of thought, strength of will and strength of heart. The power of thought is the light of knowledge, the power of will is the energy of character, the power of the heart is love. Reason, love and will are perfections, they are the highest powers, they are the absolute essence of man as man and the purpose of his existence.[5]

Feuerbach is categorical in stating that the generic essence of man and the essence of Christianity are the same. The God of Christianity and man share the same essence, which is why it can reach any people, nation or species. It is important to emphasize that the generic essence of man is the constitutive determinations of what he is as a genus and not just the properties he possesses or mere characteristics[6]. In Christianity, this essence is objectified in God, in other words, the Christian religion concentrates the qualities of the entire human race in its divinity and, in this way, as Feuerbach points out, Christianity rises above other religions

---

[5] FEUERBACH, Ludwig. *The Essence of Christianity.* [1841]. Trad. By Jose da Silva Brandao. Papirus editora. 2007, p. 36.

[6] As Aquino explains in his article *Feuerbach and the Sensible Foundation of Philosophy: Immediacy and Mediation in the I-Thou Relationship.* In: Kriterion vol. 55 n° 129, Belo Horizonte Jan/Jun 2014, p. 02.

because its God reaches the entire human race, and not just certain peoples as, for example, happened with the Pagans:

> The pagan is patriotic, the Christian is cosmopolitan, so the pagan's god is also a patriotic god, but the Christian's god is a cosmopolitan god, i.e. the pagan has a national, limited god, because the pagan didn't go beyond the boundaries of his nationality, for him the nation was above man; but the Christian has a universal, general god, who encompasses the whole universe, because he himself goes beyond the limits of nationality, he doesn't restrict human dignity and essence within a particular nation.[7]

The importance the author gives to the Christian religion, which is the closest to man and the one that has elevated him to the status of divinity, is evident. To say that it is the closest to man is to consider that it manages to affect him in a way that reaches him completely, like no other, thus revealing that both share the same essence, because only a god who is human can affect man in the way that the Christian God does.

Feuerbach, as a philosopher of sensibility, highlights love as an important element of Christian religion in the divine trinity of the essence of Christianity. God is love, that is, out of mercy he became man by being moved by human need and misery and for this reason he sacrificed his son out of compassion for man. But the philosopher, in *The Essence of Christianity*, undoes the inversion created by the religion that presents us with a God who loves, suffers, has compassion and dies for man by making us realize that God was already man even before he was God.

> Out of mercy, God became a man - he was then already a human God before he actually became a man; (...) The incarnation was a tear of divine compassion, and therefore only a phenomenon of a being who feels humanly and is therefore essentially human.[8]

The Christian religion is also the one that most elevates man to the status of divinity, because the incarnation of God in man "necessarily

---

[7] FEUERBACH. Ludwig. [1851]. *Lectures on the Essence of Religion.* Trad. By Jose da Silva Brandao. Papirus editora. 1989, p. 24.
[8] FEUERBACH, Ludwig. *The Essence of Christianity.* [1841]. Trad. By Jose da Silva Brandao. Papirus editora. 2007, p. 77.

precedes the relegation of God in man" (FEUERBACH. 2007, p. 77), since man was already in God. The human predicates were present in God even before this God was a god and later became a man, otherwise it would make no sense for him to become a man. To exemplify this thought, Feuerbach creates an illustrative and reflective passage:

> A king who does not have the welfare of his subjects in his heart (...) who is not a "common man" in his intention, as the people say, such a king will never come down bodily from his throne to gladden his people with his personal presence. So hadn't the sudite already become king before the king lowered himself to the sudite? And since the sudite feels honored and happy with the personal presence of his king, this feeling is related only to the fact itself, or rather, it is not related to the fact of the intention, the humanitarian essence, which is the reason for this fact .[9]

Therefore, from the aforementioned passage in the 1841 work, our philosopher makes us realize that the God of Christianity is only able to affect man in a complete way because he reaches his innermost being, his heart, his essence, and this is only possible because both are based on an obvious common constitution, that is, man and God only make sense to each other because they essentially share the same qualities and characteristics. Thus, the king first needed to possess the quality of a sudite in order to subsequently be a king who cares about a sudite, because he knows what it is like to be one. Therefore, the God of the Christians already possessed strictly human qualities and characteristics in his essence, even before he was divine.

Throughout his works, Feuerbach was concerned with analyzing primitive, classical Christianity, that is, not the Christianity of his time, which he already considered to be distorted and vulgar and which was shaken by the slightest breeze hanging over its fragile structure and deteriorated by refined illusions and the prejudices of old hags. In the second preface *to The Essence of Christianity,* he speaks of prejudices originating in the imagination of those who were scandalized by the publication of his greatest

---

[9] Ibidem, p. 77-88.

work. In this sense, the philosopher adds:

> No wonder, then, that the age of apparent, illusory, infamous Christianity has been so scandalized by *The Essence of Christianity*. Christianity has already become so distorted and disused that even the erudite official representatives of Christianity, the theologians, no longer know or at least don't want to know what Christianity is .[10]

The objections raised against his work are rigorously refuted on the basis of testimonies in books, illustrations and documents, which are the irrefutable historical and empirical evidence in a faithful and correct translation of the Christian religion.

In the first part of *The Essence of Christianity*, Feuerbach describes what is positive about religion; in the second part, what is negative. He refers to what is affirmative in classical Christianity (note, Christianity before it was theologized), by observing that this religion is an expression of universality, of genre, and that from it its predicates, which actually belong to man, are recognized as something divine, perfect and infinite, when Christianity describes the human essence of religion.

> For this reason, it is divided into two parts, the first of which is affirmative, the second (including the appendix) negative, not totally, but for the most part; in both, however, the same thing is demonstrated, only in a different or even opposite way. The first is the solution of religion in its essence, in its truth, the second the solution of it in its contradictions; the first development, the second polemic; the former, by the very nature of the subject, more tranquil, the latter more lively .[11]

The true essence of religion is anthropological, i.e. through religion we can get to know everything that humanity is. In this way, through a religious archaeology we will get to know what a certain people is, according to its beliefs, its desires, its longings, and as Feuerbach says, its most intimate secrets of love. What follows in his magnum opus is also what he considers negative in Christian religion: the false essence that appears when religion

---

[10] FEUERBACH, Ludwig. *The Essence of Christianity*. [1841]. Trad. By Jose da Silva Brandao. Papirus editora. 2007, p. 19.
[11] FEUERBACH, Ludwig. *The Essence of Christianity*. [1841]. Trad. By Jose da Silva Brandao. Papirus editora. 2007, p. 23.

becomes theology and man is alienated from his essence.

Alienation from a certain point of view is making someone else alien, transferring what is one's own to someone else. In religion, as Feuerbach repeatedly points out, man alienates himself, makes alien to himself that which makes him exactly what he is, that is, his generic human essence, which ends up being harmfully concentrated in a single idea that dominates him, making him passive in a relationship in which he submits in the most bestial way to the idolized object. Sacrifices, cults and exploitation are justified in the name of the object of worship, which is precisely why the German philosopher tries to unveil the mysteries concealed by the sacred cloak of ignorance and despair. Feuerbach almost exclusively devotes his entire philosophy to this object of study, religious sentiment and everything that stems from it.

The most attentive reader of Feuerbach's works will notice that his preoccupation with the subject of religion has never been more topical than at this moment in our history. When Feuerbach reveals, in his lectures of 1851, that his goal is to clarify the minds of those who are dominated and manipulated by other men through religion, which is established as an effective instrument of domination, the philosopher seemed to be trying to solve a current problem.

> I am interested above all, and always have been, in illuminating the obscure essence of religion with the light of reason, so that men can finally stop being exploited, so that they can stop being the playthings of all those powers that are enemies of humanity and which, as always, have used the cloudiness of religion to oppress man.[12]

The author's concern is with religion, or even mainly theology, which for him would be rationalized religion. Some might disagree with Feuerbach in this sense, since he identifies religion or theology as the means by which

---

[12] FEUERBACH. Ludwig. [1851]. *Lectures on the Essence of Religion*. Trad. By Jose da Silva Brandao. Papirus editora. 1989, p. 28.

men exploit each other, or, as was said earlier, an effective instrument of domination that promotes the highest degree of submission of those who seek solace and consolation for the terrible hardships of life. By saying that it is not God or religion that promotes such absurdities, but the questionable conduct of certain men who are false religionists, we are only looking at the problem from a partial perspective.

This simple and naïve thought is easily deconstructed when analyzed through Feuerbachian optics, when the author dives deep into the essence of religion and man. According to Feuerbach, there is a contradiction in the very essence of religion: faith and love, which are responsible for the absurdities already described.

Present in chapter XXVII *of The Essence of Christianity*, this theme is possibly the most important element that leads us to an undoubted understanding of how theology denies man. There is a dichotomy between faith and love. One cannot exist if the other already exists in the same context. This dichotomy refers to the inevitable contradiction between faith, which is pure subjectivity, and love, which is pure objectivity. In this way, Feuerbach develops an argument that transforms the foundations of Christian religion into a conflict between the objective and the subjective.

We can understand that man in a general sense is denied through faith, since faith, a requirement of any religion, is the link between man and God and, consequently, it is a point of distance between man and another man. Therefore, faith, the supreme necessity of theology, first brings man closer to God and then separates him from man.

Feuerbach explains throughout the present chapter in *The Essence of Christianity* that faith determines truth, and in due course this truth determined by it refers to what it has determined by arbitrarily and in due course attributing it as truth to everyone: God is the true one and must be praised and worshipped.

> Faith has a specific, special truth, which is therefore necessarily linked to denial in its content. Faith is by nature exclusive. There is only one truth, only one God, only one to whom the monopoly of the Son of God belongs; everything else is nothing, it is error, illusion.[13]

Faith is not revealed to all ordinary people without distinction. On the contrary, the path that leads man to faith is special and therefore also leads him to his object of worship, which is also special, that is, his God. This being the case, only distinguished men who sacrifice themselves fully and truly are capable of attaining it. In this way, we necessarily notice that there is always a demand that leads man down a unique, special path, which distances him from humanity, from the general, leading him to the particular. This denies the genre itself in favor of something particular, strict and limited. In this way, the appreciation of the other is compromised, because faith takes for itself everything that belongs to the other, in other words, everything that is objective, nature, everything that is appropriated by it and concentrated in its fundamental object, God, in a sovereign and haughty way.

Faith is proud, and this pride is evident in the one who makes use of it, the believer. He is not an ordinary man, he is different from others because he is special. His distinction is due to the fact that this particular man overcomes the limits of nature, denying everything that refers to it. The believer is different from the rest because he is linked through faith to the ultimate object of his worship, God.

> Faith gives man a special sense of honor and of himself. The believer thinks of himself as excellent before other men, elevated above the natural man; he only knows himself as a person of distinction, in possession of special rights; believers are aristocrats and unbelievers plebeians. God is this personified difference and the privilege of the believer before the unbeliever.[14]

From this point of view, Feuerbach in his detailed analysis presents

---

[13] FEUERBACH, Ludwig. *The Essence of Christianity*. [1841]. Trad. By Jose da Silva Brandao. Papirus editora. 1988, p. 246.
[14] FEUERBACH, Ludwig. *The Essence of Christianity*. [1841]. Trad. By Jose da Silva Brandao. Papirus editora. 1988, p. 248.

the other side of faith, the opposite of what is traditionally presented by theology. Faith sets the particular man above the rest, because he is special and full of honor. However, this honor does not refer to this man himself, but to another, to an equally special being in whom he mirrors himself. This is because faith imagines its essence as belonging to this other special being, God. So the particular man, the believer, puts his honor, his pride and everything that elevates him above others onto the other being, not directly onto himself.

Even though faith makes believers special in relation to others, it makes their negation possible. It annuls even the particular man because it transforms him as an active being into a theologically passive man, that is, it reduces the natural forces vital to every human being, not just the believer, into passive activity, an activity only of feeling trapped in the realm of subjectivity.

> In short, we have here the characteristic principle of religion, that it is the natural active transformed into a passive. The pagan is elevated, the Christian feels elevated. The Christian transforms into a matter of feeling, of sensitivity, what for the pagan is a matter of natural activity .[15]

The Christian believer, even in what should make him positively different from the common man, contradictorily and without realizing it, transforms the core of Christian doctrine, that is, humility, into something negative. Negative because, in a hidden way, humility is not what it should apparently be. In fact, its opposite is pride: "The humility of the believer is pride in reverse - a pride that has no appearances, the outward signs of pride" (FEUERBACH. 2007, p. 248).

This pride that is embedded in humility is not
It is not easily identified. Not even the believer realizes that the
humility, the core of Christian doctrine, consists of a contradiction. The believer himself is victimized by it. It is not his fault. The contradiction

---

[15] Ibid.

present in humility, that is, the fact that it shows itself outwardly as a virtue, but consists of exactly what it most repudiates, that is, its opposite, pride, necessarily manifests itself to make the one who has it as a virtue a distinct and special person in relation to others. And the believer is not to blame for this simply because he doesn't realize it. Thus, "he does not make himself in general the goal of his own activity, but the goal, the object of God" (FEUERBACH. 2007, p. 248).

The believer acts according to what is determined by faith. It determines what is right and what must be followed, thus subjecting the believer to its demands. Faith is the structural element of everything that comes from religion, it is something that must first be attained and maintained in order for the object worshipped to subsist, because if it is not admitted above all else, if it is not the first element to be accepted by religious man, all the other elements of divine order will make no sense, namely everything that is in the envelope of religion. Faith is something extremely determined. Determination is a necessary requirement of its essence, because if there is faith there is faith in something that has to be determined and specific:

> Faith is essentially a determined faith. God is the true God only in this determination. This Jesus is Christ, the true, only prophet, the only-begotten son of God. And in this determinate one you must believe if you don't want to lose your happiness [16]

Faith is not only something determined, as has already been explained, but it is also imperative. Its imperativeness consists in the fact that religious man is required to be what it determines, i.e. if you don't believe in divinity you are against it, because faith accepts no middle ground. There is no freedom to challenge what it determines through its dogma. The establishment of this dogma is the first step to be taken, because it is from this that the others arise.

---

[16] FEUERBACH, Ludwig. *The Essence of Christianity.* [1841]. Trad. By Jose da Silva Brandao. Papirus editora. 1988, p. 249.

> The fact that, once a fundamental dogma has been established, special issues are linked to it that must then be decided dogmatically, and that this results in a tedious multiplicity of dogmas, is certainly an inevitability, but it does not negate the need for faith to be fixed in dogmas so that it knows what it must believe and how it can achieve its happiness.[17]

Dogma is the starting point for other dogmas that arise to guide the conduct of believers in various aspects of their lives. But dogma only expresses what faith has already foreseen, that is, dogma only exists because of faith. It is a necessary expression that will underpin faith, even though it is a presupposition to it.

Feuerbach finds in the determinates of faith

The fact that faith is based on its dogmas is an important point in separating believers from non-believers in the same divine being. By determining something, faith makes it impossible, as has already been discussed, for there to be any middle ground. There is no freedom in faith: you are either a Christian or an anti-Christian. It is from this determination that the philosopher notes the limitation of faith.

But the limitation of faith is dealt with in a convenient, timely manner by religion. The limitation that comes from determination and its immediate consequence, delimitation, is opposed to the biblical texts and, through the arbitrariness of exegesis, a convenient interpretation manages to "overcome" the limits of the dogmas. In other words, what was determined by the faith through its dogmas, these, when shown to be something limited, poor, that no longer satisfies the believing man, become different in the most convenient way possible.

> It is only the lack of character, the unbelieving believer of recent times who hides behind the Bible and opposes biblical sayings to dogmatic determinations in order, through the arbitrariness of exegesis, to free himself from the limits of dogmatics. But faith has already disappeared, it has already become different when the determinations of faith are already

---

[17] FEUERBACH, Ludwig. *The Essence of Christianity.* [1841]. Trad. By Jose da Silva Brandao. Papirus editora. 1988, p. 249.

felt as limitations.[18]

In this way, we can understand that faith is not even fixed on what it is committed to. On the contrary, under the pretext of believing in what is essential to it, it ends up believing in what is vague and undefined. "(...) instead of the determined Son of God, characteristic of the Church, it establishes a vague determination, which like no other could be called the Son of God" (FEUERBACH. 2007, p. 249-50).

Belief, Feuerbach points out, becomes synonymous with being good and, to return to what has been said, faith leaves no room for middle ground. Therefore, not believing is the same as being bad and, consequently, this argument falls into the most perverse subjectivity, which is represented by intention. The unbeliever, in intention, is an evil man because he is an enemy of Christ, the supreme good. Faith is selective among humans, because it chooses for itself only those who make use of it, and it reserves repulsion and evil for unbelievers. Faith isolates men, denying those who are not in its favor, arbitrarily judging them as enemies deserving of the most terrible punishments: "Blessed, dear to God, partakers of eternal happiness are the believers, cursed, expelled from God and repudiated by man are the unbelievers, for what God repudiates man cannot accept, cannot spare" (FEUERBACH. 1988, p. 251).

The cruel side of faith is also analyzed by Feuerbach, who sees as a consequence of all that has been exposed a contradiction with what, in the case of Christian religion, should be synonymous, but is presented as its opposite, that is, faith proves to be contradictory to love.

Faith separates people, nullifies their generic essence, while love unites them. Christianity is the religion of love, but the love presented to us by Christianity is a limited love, i.e. there is only love between those who are already Christians or who may one day become Christians. In this sense, it

---

[18] I FEUERBACH, Ludwig. *The Essence of Christianity*. [1841]. Trad. By Jose da Silva Brandao. Papirus editora. 1988, p. 249-50.

is necessary to quote the author: "The Christian can then only love the Christian, or another only as a potential Christian; he can only love what faith consecrates, embraces. Faith is the baptism of love" (FEUERBACH. 2007, p. 251).

If the love of Christianity only reaches those who through faith are or can become Christians, then this peculiar kind of love is limited. Feuerbach disregards such love as love, because for the philosopher a love based on a special phenomenon contradicts the essence of love, which is unlimited. The essence of love can only be limited by reason and surpasses the limits of any condition that restricts it to certain specialties. Feuerbach makes it clear in his ethical proposal that love rises above Christian religion, which ironically is considered to be the religion of love, but not of love in an essential, generic sense, but in a particular one:

> We must love man for man. Man is the object of love because he is an object in himself, because he is a rational being fit for love. This is the law of the genre, the law of intelligence. Love must be an immediate love, yes, it is only love as long as it is immediate .[19]

In this way, faith nullifies man, denies him in the name of a divine object that is actually part of him. And in this way it alienates him from his essence, from his gender, because he doesn't recognize himself as a complete man, since this capacity for self-recognition has already been taken away from him. In theology, through faith, man is an essentially dependent and incomplete creature, half animal, half angel. Feuerbach borrows these terms from religion to explain the goal of his philosophy, and from this understanding we can conclude that the goal of faith in religion is not what it appears to be, but on the contrary, it ends up transforming man into a null being who does not exist for himself, but for the object created by him.

---

[19] FEUERBACH, Ludwig. *The Essence of Christianity.* [1841]. Trad. By Jose da Silva Brandao. Papirus editora. 1988, p. 263.

Therefore, in *The Essence of Christianity*, the religious question is analyzed from an anthropological point of view, in which Feuerbach analyzes the human race in order to arrive at what is the basis of religion, its deepest and most intimate foundation, its essence. Thus, he deals with this issue as no other author has dared to do before, living up to the meaning of its author's name "stream of fire". Throughout his most famous work, the philosopher at no point bases religion on nothing, even though the object of study is not a concrete entity such as a form of knowledge. For him, even if religion is just a kind of fanciful knowledge about man, it is still a valid source of knowledge, which differs from the treatment it has received from other philosophers such as the English empiricists, for example.

> When we go through our libraries, convinced of these principles, what destruction we have to do! Let's take in our hands any volume of theology or metaphysics, for example, and ask: does it contain any abstract reasoning relating to quantity and number? No. Does it contain any experimental reasoning concerning factual materials and experience? No. Throw it in the fire, then, because it contains nothing but sophistry and illusions.[20]

Contrary to this, Feuerbach affirms that religion, although it is in the realm of fantasy or dreams of the human mind, nevertheless, in dreams, we do not find ourselves in a void; on the contrary, we are in the realm of reality. Feuerbach's view of religion in his 1841 work is the product of a thorough analysis carried out using a method that he himself calls historico-philosophical. In this method, he uses an approach to the historical events of religion. However, a mere historical analysis of religious facts would prove insufficient to fully explain the religious phenomenon.

A historical analysis would only be concerned with demonstrating whether or not a given religious fact had occurred, thus sticking to the historical evidence which is only analyzed from the closed and self-sufficient point of view of science. Feuerbach criticizes this type of analysis, because

---

[20] FEUERBACH, Ludwig. *The Essence of Christianity*. [1841]. Trad. By Jose da Silva Brandao. Papirus editora. 1988, p.09.

once the impossibility of a miracle has been verified, religion would be considered a mere mental illusion or deception. In other words, this type of analysis would not answer the religious question in a complete way, it would only reduce religion to a product of imagination. Therefore, the big issue that cannot be seen from this kind of point of view is the fact that

> History cannot be understood as a collection of raw facts to be verified according to positivist canons. It is more than that. History is the arena in which the human essence expresses itself. And for this very reason, all the products of imagination have a meaning.[21]

Throughout *The Essence of Christianity*, it can be seen that what Feuerbach does is place religion as something based on man himself, on what essentially grounds him. The generic essence of man is what is most intimate, defines and grounds him. It is made up of three indispensable elements for his existence: heart, will and reason. These elements are absolute and perfect, due to the fact that they are ends in themselves.

> Man exists to know, to love and to want. But what is the purpose of reason? Reason. Love? Love. Will? Free will.
> We know in order to know, we love in order to love, we want in order to want, i.e. in order to be free. The true essence is the one that thinks, that loves, that desires.[22]

Will, reason and heart fully realize man as a genus, in other words, they make him what he is, because without them man would be nothing. These elements are only determined by themselves, that is, by their very essence. This is equivalent to saying that when man becomes aware of any object, be it in the realm of will, reason or heart, at the same time he becomes aware of its essence.

> Feeling is only determined by the sentimental, i.e. by itself, by its very essence. Likewise will and reason. So whatever object we become aware of will make us aware of our own essence; we can't confirm anything without confirming ourselves. And because willing, feeling and thinking are perfections,

---

[21] FEUERBACH, Ludwig. *The Essence of Christianity.* [1841]. Trad. By Jose da Silva Brandao. Papirus editora. 1988,p. 12.
[22] Ibidem, p. 45.

essences, realities, it is impossible to perceive or feel reason with reason, feeling with feeling, will with will as a limited, finite, i.e. null force .[23]

The book's historical analysis seeks to interpret each religious fact as an expression of the human essence in history. This type of historical-philosophical analysis can also be found throughout his Lectures *on the Essence of Religion*, although the object of study, although the same, religion, differs in its approach.

In his 1841 work, *The Essence of Christianity*, he devotes himself to questions concerning the human race and all its perfection. The religion he deals with, Christianity, is critically analyzed only in the moral, i.e. human, sense of this particular religion. When, almost ten years later, he tries to respond to the criticism of his first work, for referring to man without anything preceding him and for disregarding nature, then, in defense of his greatest work, he argues that Christianity itself has disregarded it, since, "Christianity is idealism, establishing at the top a god without nature (...) for having then dealt in The Essence of Christianity only with the essence of man" (Feuerbach. 1988). But in *The Essence of Christianity*, what the author proposed was achieved, since the mysteries were revealed and religion, from this work onwards, can be understood in a way like never before.

1.2   The Foundations of Religion in *Lectures on the Essence of Religion*

In his book *Prelegoes on the Essence of Religion* (1848-51), Feuerbach offers a psychological explanation that differs from the anthropological analysis of the same question. The reason that makes God a personified being and distinct from man is due to the insufficient relationship he has with what is most powerful and external to him: nature.

---

[23] Ibidem, p. 47.

Once personified, the forces of nature take the form of supernatural, extraordinary beings that provoke in man the most diverse and even contradictory feelings such as fear, security, gratitude and benevolence. But these feelings are based on the greatest of all feelings, not the only one, but the main one that is responsible for them: the feeling of dependence which, according to

Feuerbach, is fundamental to the existence of religion.

> When we consider the religions of both the so-called savages, about whom travelers instruct us, and the cultivated peoples, when we penetrate into our own direct intimacy, unfailingly accessible to observation, we find no other psychological explanation as proper and complete as the feeling or awareness of dependence[24]

For theology, the feeling of dependence is established in man in relation to God, in other words, everything that man is, he can only be if the divine allows it. Man comes to depend on God's will and benevolence in order to guarantee his survival in the natural world and also in a supra-natural world. But for Feuerbach, this dependence is actually on nature and nothing else; nature is the only being on which man really depends in order to exist.

So is nature the true divine being? Not really, because man can depend on it without the need for exaggerated worship, nothing in the mystical or superstitious sense. Feuerbach affirms that theology and anthropology are the being through which nature is personified, becoming conscious and intelligent, and this being is man.

By stating that theology is anthropology, the philosopher once again reminds us of a constant throughout his philosophy: "all our thinking about God is thinking about ourselves" (Rubem Alves. Back cover of Prelegoes sobre a Essencia da Religiao: 1988). At this point in his lectures, the author

---

[24] FEUERBACH. Ludwig. [1851]. *Lectures on the Essence of Religion.* Trad. By Jose da Silva Brandao. Papirus editora. 1989, p. 30.

explains why humanity has so many gods. But what would be the fundamental principle to explain this enormous variety of divinities?

Feuerbach always uses the same argument to explain the existence of God: God is the essence of man divinized. So how could he explain this variety of gods in polytheism, if humanity is only one? In order to proceed with this explanation, we must first remember that, for the philosopher, religion is one of humanity's first forms of culture, and as a culture it expresses, albeit in an infantile way, all the thought of a people. Peoples are many, and peoples are as diverse as their gods. Peoples are as diverse as their needs, i.e. the people who worship the rain god because they depend on it to live, the people who worship a particular animal because it is necessary for their life, i.e. even the feeling of dependence differs in terms of the species in relation to the object that is vital for their existence, but it is the same in terms of gender.

What Feuerbach means is that the difference between polytheism and monotheism is only the difference between species and genus. There are several species, while the genus is only one, i.e. monotheistic religions refer to the human genus while polytheistic religions refer to different peoples, and are therefore considered by him to be national religions attached to a particular culture.

> Polytheism only exists where man has not yet risen above the concept of the human species, where he only recognizes the man of his species as his fellow man of equal right and equal ability. But in the concept of species there is multiplicity, so there are many gods where man makes the essence of the species an absolute essence. Monotheism, however, reaches man the moment he rises to the concept of the genus, in which all men are equal, where their differences of species, race and nationality disappear.

It is therefore quite clear that, for Feuerbach, in the Lectures *on the Essence of Religion,* the feeling of[25] FEUERBACH. Ludwig. [1851]. *Lectures on the Essence of Religion.* Trad. By Jose da Silva Brandao. Papirus editora. 1989, p. 24.

dependence is the basis of religion, a universal concept that explains the subjective and psychological foundation of religion. It is the foundation, but it is not the only feeling responsible for religion. After all, before anything else, man loves himself and only fears something that could take away from him what he most desires, but what does he most desire? Life? To continue living at any cost in this world where he finds himself alone and exposed to the hardships of nature and its needs? Is that what makes him create God, to try to overcome his limited abilities?

Man doesn't want to live at all costs; first and foremost, he wants to be happy, even if he has to deny what he cherishes most: life. Feuerbach finds in man an instinct that seeks happiness, which he considers to be the instinct of instincts that takes precedence over all others, even over the instinct for self-preservation. It is notable that man only worships God because he loves himself, after all God is also love and all the feelings that somehow bring good to man, whether directly or indirectly, that is, there is an egoism in man, in the sense of self-love, which precedes the feeling of dependence, because it is only because of this that man worships God or everything that brings him good.

Therefore, from Lectures *on the Essence of Religion* we can understand how the most diverse and contradictory feelings arise in man, since these feelings are fundamental to the existence and maintenance of religious belief. Throughout the lectures, we are introduced to man in a way that the author had not done before, in order to understand human feelings in relation to nature. This way, this work exposes the psychological impressions that nature imprints on man more than the previous one.

1.3 The Foundation of Religion in Feuerbach

In both works, it is notable that Feuerbach deals with the same subject, the foundation of religion, from different perspectives. In *The*

Essence of Christianity he makes an anthropological analysis of the foundation of religion, while in *Preleoges on the Essence of Religion* there is a very timely psychological explanation of the relationship between man and nature. The latter states that the feeling of dependence is one of the reasons behind man's belief in and worship of gods. While in the first work cited there is a more objective analysis in which the perfection of the human race is highlighted, based on the essences (will, reason and heart) as the foundations of the human essence and consequently of the essence of religion. But is there really a difference in the author's opinion on the foundations of religion? Or does one work end up complementing the other, even in different ways?

In the first work, *The Essence of Christianity*, Feuerbach treats Christian religion and its relationship with the human race as his object of study and, in the subsequent book, *Prelegoes on the Essence of Religion*, written after a seven-year break, the study turns to the psychological impressions that man's relationship with nature provokes in him. Man's feeling of dependence on nature is the main, but not the only, basis of religion. In this second work, nature becomes the main element of study for Feuerbach and all the feelings it arouses in human beings.

On the one hand, we find a Feuerbach who shows the full magnitude of man by referring to the human race with nothing preceding it and bearing a perfect, absolute and infinite generic essence. Because of this, he is accused of radical anthropocentrism, "(...) that is why it was thought that I had allowed the human essence to emerge from nothing, making it a being that presupposes nothing, and that contradicted my supposed divinization of man (...)" (Feuerbach, 1989, p.26) and on the other hand, after seven years of isolation in the countryside, we have a Feuerbach who, in the course of his work, uses a psychological description to present a man with a feeling of finitude and dependence on nature, as he is at the mercy of its storms, making these the starting point of religious sentiment "The feeling of dependence is the only universally certain name and concept for designating and explaining the psychological and subjective foundation of religion". (FEUERBACH.Ludwig. 1988, p. 35).

So don't these divergent points of view demonstrate a contradiction to the most important question of his entire philosophy: what underlies the existence of religion. What makes man believe in gods, why do they appear in human life? Is it due to fear and feelings of finitude or dependence, aroused by man's relationship with nature, or simply the perfection of the human race? The human race, as we well know, even dominates and controls nature, radically contradicting the first theory seen in the lectures? The problematic for the question has been launched and what is most important to know is whether or not the philosopher has a different view of man that may have emerged in the time between one work and another.

In short, the problem of the issue is presented in a cautious manner so as not to reach a false conclusion or even a forced reconciliation between the two works. Interpreting Feuerbach's thought thus proves to be a somewhat arduous and dangerous task, as one runs the risk of saying what the philosopher didn't say on this controversial subject. Religion looms large over the development of human history and demonstrates enormous strength even today.

Thus, the philosopher's intention throughout his works is to try to promote a recovery of man, of the human essence that has been appropriated by religion and concentrated in a single object, God. In seeking to rescue the human essence, Feuerbach commits himself to an objective that aims both to prepare a human model of reason and to escape from the paradigms established in modernity, from the prevalence of technical-scientific thinking and an abstract metaphysics, by creating an integral conception of the human being. This Feuerbachian project truly consists of a mixture whose measure is established in an egalitarian way without one of these elements prevailing over the other. In this sense, Adriana Verissimo

Serrao explains that:

> (...) Feuerbach's thought is mobilized by a central intuition, which must even be considered with its unique problem: the simultaneous establishment of a *human model of reason* and an integral conception of the human being .[25]

From this perspective, we can see that the author's intention is to diagnose man as suffering from an unrecognized pathology that diminishes him in order to arbitrarily magnify the one who, in fact, depends on him to exist. Throughout his philosophy, Feuerbach tries to overcome the dehumanization of man, whether it comes from theology, which alienates him from his own essence, from metaphysics, which transforms him into a mere abstract being, or from science itself, which transforms him into a simple instrumentalized object. In all these conditions, man is alienated, expropriated from what he is in the name of something that, although dependent on him to exist, is inverted in a relationship in which the subject becomes the predicate and the predicate becomes the subject, annulling or giving rise to a broken man, split in himself.

Feuerbachian philosophy emerged as a necessary response to Hegelianism. For Feuerbach, Hegelian philosophy makes it possible to grasp the idea of thinking about the individual and subjectivity in their relationship with the whole, the spirit or how it expresses the genre. On the other hand, the Hegelian system causes ambiguity in the way it presents religion. Hegel and his right-wing disciples leave philosophy and religion in a peaceful coexistence, that is, the philosophy of Hegel and his first-order disciples only establishes a rational, systematic and absolute justification for religion through speculative juggling. Hegel promotes, according to Feuerbach, an arbitrary symbiosis of other philosophies passed on by translation without any truly positive force because he doesn't deny enough

---

[25] SERRAO, Adriana Verissimo. *The Humanity of Reason - Ludwig Feuerbach and the Project of an Integral Anthropology.* Lisbon: Calouste Gulbenkian Foundation. 1999, p. 20.

of what has already been enshrined, he just preserves it.

> (...) for some it is or seems necessary to preserve the old and banish what is new; for others it is imperative to realize the new. (...) The need for preservation is only an artificial, created need - it is only a reaction. Hegelian philosophy was the arbitrary synthesis of various existing systems, of insufficiencies - without positive force, because without absolute negativity. Only those who have the courage to be absolutely negative have the strength to create novelty.[26]

In order for Feuerbach to propose the rescue of man's essence-genre, he first had to undo the inversion created by religion and also by Hegel's well-founded and structured speculative philosophy. Feuerbach had the arduous, daring and also dangerous task of striking at the heart of both religion and Hegel's idealist philosophy.

---

[26] FEUERBACH, Ludwig. *The Essence of Christianity*. [1841]. Trad. By Jose da Silva Brandao. Papirus editora. 1988, p. 14.

CHAPTER 2: THE GENERIC ESSENCE OF MAN

In the previous chapter, the problematic existing in the two works was exposed. It sought to compare the anthropological or objective perspective present in The *Essence of Christianity* with the psychological or subjective perspective of the *Lectures on the Essence of Religion*, so that it would be possible to see that the arguments used by Feuerbach to explain the fundamental principle of religion are distinct or even contrary. This second chapter will define the main concepts of Feuerbachian philosophy that are necessary for a better understanding of religion. The first sub-chapter, 2.1 *Man in Feuerbach,* conceptualizes man as he is expressed in *The Essence of Christianity, and* the second, 2.2 *Consciousness,* deals with what differentiates man from all other beings. The chapter concludes with the subchapter
2.3   Feuerbach's *Objectivation Theory is based* on the importance of man's relationship with objects, since it is objects that enable man to know his own essence.

2.1 Man in Feuerbach

In order to understand what religion is, the object of study of this research, according to Feuerbachian optics, we must first understand what man is. To this end, it is of the utmost importance to explain the difference between man in his general sense and man in his individual sense, so that we can then understand the importance Feuerbach attaches to the human essence and its relationship to religion and what underpins it.

When Feuerbach talks about man in his strictly individual sense, he is referring to the human individual himself, who is sensitive, corporeal, limited and imperfect. However, when he deals with man, so to speak, in the broad generic sense, in the human totality, he is consequently referring to that which is responsible for the perfection of his own essence. In other words, man in the generic sense is visibly the opposite of individual man, the former being the real bearer of the divine predicates that are radically opposed to the latter.

The human race, as described by Feuerbach in *The Essence of Christianity*, consists of an essence of the totality of individuals, but this does not mean that it is the sum total of all its members. In fact, it is a single, universal and infinite essence, as the author describes in his youthful thesis[27]. This essence manifests itself in time and in each specific individual, amounting only to a particularization. In Feuerbach's view, the human race is not the result of the quantity of individuals who perfect themselves over time on the basis of the different qualities that exist between each of them; on the contrary, the human race is perfection itself, precisely because it consists not of a multiplicity, but of an infinite and perfect unity, which is precisely why it is sufficient in itself.

> The human race, which is not a summative totality of individuals but the summative essence of that same totality, remains indifferent to the quantitative multiplicity of individuals and is not enriched by the qualitative diversity of its members [28]

In *The Essence of Christianity*, Feuerbach describes man from an anthropological point of view that is objectified in the world and which, as the bearer of essences that are perfect in themselves, elevates man to the status of a divine being, that is, man in his generic sense, not in his individual, subjective sense as described by the author in his lectures of 1851. So, as has been said in this research so far, is it in the condition of man's generic perfection that lies at the heart of the awakening of religious sentiment in human beings? Is this condition the fundamental factor behind

---

[27] *On the One, Universal and Infinite Reason* was the thesis developed by Feuerbach in 1828 for his doctorate. In it, he argues that the unity of men expresses nothing more than *the unity of reason itself* "unitas hominum nihil aliud exprimat signicetque, quam *unitatem rationis ipsius*". (SERRAO, Adriana Verissimo. *The Humanity of Reason - Ludwig Feuerbach and the Project of an Integral Anthropology*. Lisbon: Calouste Gulbenkian Foundation. 1999, p. 31.)
[28] FEUERBACH, Ludwig. *The Essence of Christianity*. [1841]. Trad. By Jose da Silva Brandao. Papirus editora. 1988, p. 43.

Feuerbach's treatment of religious sentiment as an innate or at least essential feeling in every human being?

In order to delve deeper into these issues, it is necessary to understand how Landshut's philosopher conceives of the perfection of the human race and its divinization through religion, since the author deals with this issue that has already been dealt with by previous philosophers, including Rene Descartes (1596-1650). As will be discussed below, from an objective or anthropological point of view, we avoid the particularities of subjectivism, which isolates man by not allowing him to see his gender.

To say that Feuerbach analyzes the perfection of the human genre in an objective way consists of the idea of overcoming the solipsistic self described by Descartes throughout his meditations and the consequent elaboration of a conceptual configuration of the genre *(Gattung)* based on real man and not on metaphysical speculations. The generic human essence is constituted by the triad that is unveiled, defining it as such. As explained above, reason, will and heart are one and the same essence within the unity of consciousness that is shared in the coming together of individuals, but not as a merely summative condition, as has already been made clear.

Throughout *The Essence of Christianity,* Feuerbach presents us with a very objective view of man. To say that his point of view is objective means that he makes an anthropological analysis taking into account very little, if any, form of subjectivity when it comes to the human race. The German philosopher also disregards what presupposes man, since he describes him without showing us anything that precedes him. The author presents us with a man without a determined origin, but he will only concern himself with this question, the origin of man and everything that surrounds him, in his lectures of 1851, when he finally addresses the question of man's interaction with nature, as he himself admits in the third lecture of the 1841 work:

> (...) Because in *The Essence of Christianity* I dealt only with the *essence* of man, beginning my work immediately with it (...) it was thought that I had allowed the human essence to emerge from nothing, making it a being that presupposes nothing and that contradicts nothing with my supposed divinization of man (...)[29]

The man exposed in his most famous work, *The Essence of Christianity*, is divided between the individual and the genus. By approaching man in his generic sense, which is above the individual, Feuerbach deals with a significant aspect of his entire philosophy: the perfection of the genus. The human race is shown to be unlimited, absolute, infinite, that is to say, the bearer of all the qualities of perfection that are present in its God, because it is sufficient in itself, it is absolute.

> Every being is enough for itself. No being can deny itself, i.e. deny its essence; no being is limited to itself. On the contrary, every being is infinite *in itself* and *for itself*; it has its God, the highest essence in itself. Every limitation of a being exists only for another being beyond and above it.[30]

Feuerbach finds in the human genus the objectification of the human essence. Man as a genus expresses exactly all the perfection of his essence. The reason he identifies the human essence as something perfect is that it is finality in itself. This means that what defines him as man is enough for himself. Not only is the human essence perfect for him, but the essence of any other being also becomes perfect because it does not go beyond what is necessary for its existence. Even the life of a microbe demonstrates this perfection to which the author refers:

> The life of microbes is extremely short compared to that of animals that live longer; however, for them this short life is as long as for others the life of years. The leaf on which the caterpillar lives is for it a world, an infinite space. (...) How would it be possible to perceive its being as non-being, its

---

[29] FEUERBACH. Ludwig. [1851]. *Lectures on the Essence of Religion*. Trad. By Jose da Silva Brandao. Papirus editora. 1989, p. 25.
[30] FEUERBACH. Ludwig. [1841]. *The Essence of Christianity*. Trad. By Jose da Silva Brandao. Papirus editora. 1988, p. 49.

> wealth as poverty, its talent as incapacity? If plants had eyes, taste and judgment - each plant would choose its flower as the most beautiful, because its taste would not go beyond the essential productive capacity. (...) What essence affirms, reason, taste or judgment cannot deny; otherwise it would no longer be the reason and judgment of a determined being, but of any being. The measure of a being is also the measure of intelligence. If being is limited, then feeling and reason are also limited. But for a limited being, limited intelligence is not a limitation; on the contrary, he feels completely happy and satisfied with it (...) [31]

Feuerbach considers man to be a being who is grounded[32] by an essence, according to him, a complete man is grounded by will, reason and heart, this is the human essence. The human essence is perfect because it is final in itself.

> But what is the essence of man, of which he is conscious, or what realizes the genre, the very humanity of man? Reason, will and heart. A complete man possesses the power of thought, the power of will and the power of the heart.[33]

These three elements are exactly what fulfill the purpose of human existence. They are perfect in themselves, because they have their purpose in themselves. But how can the man who is grounded in this essence, that is, the man who is only what he is because of these elements, not be something absolute, perfect, if each of these elements in itself is already something perfect? How is it possible for something perfect to infinitely reach error, deception and become limited?

When describing the essence of man as something perfect, because it is finality in itself, for example: the finality of reason is rationality itself, of love is love, of will is free will, Feuerbach is referring only to what is internal and secret to man and when he says that man is not an absolute being, he is referring to man as an individual being, of nature which depends on it in everything, in other words, everything that is external to man and not of his essence in the general sense that is internal to him.

---

[31] FEUERBACH. Ludwig. [1841]. *The Essence of Christianity*. Trad. By Jose da Silva Brandao. Papirus editora. 1988, p. 49.
[32] This word is used by the author on page 45, I. 14.
[33] Ibidem, p. 44.

2.2 Consciousness

Man is a being who differs in essence from all others by the simple and common fact that he possesses that which elevates him to the status of a specific being: consciousness. But what is consciousness, this all-important characteristic that distinguishes us from all other beings? In Feuerbach's strict sense, consciousness is the ability of a being to have its own gender as its object. Man possesses this capacity not only because he can recognize himself, but also the other: *Consciousness in the strict sense exists only when, for a being, its genus, its quality, is the object* (FEUERBACH, 1988). Man is able to recognize the other and have him for himself as an object of knowledge. This means that man is able to put himself in the place of the other, turning what is external to him into something that is internal to him, in other words, having the I and the Thou for himself, because not only is his individuality an object for him, but also his own gender.

Feuerbach identifies this relationship between I and Thou as the main difference between man and other animals, after all, animals can only recognize their individuality and man cannot. Man manages to go beyond this, thus exercising what the author defines as a legitimate gender function that is expressed in speaking and thinking without the need for the other. To say that animals recognize themselves in the context of their individuality is the same as saying that they are conscious only of themselves. Therefore, in order to avoid the most foolish misunderstandings about the consciousness of animals, it is necessary to explain that, for the philosopher, this certain type of consciousness that animals possess only refers to what allows them to act in the immediacy of the situation and to sensorially discern everything around them. Such action is limited to what is in a sensory ambit, the perception of objects through their sense organs, including making judgments about things that are external to them, but without ever having them for themselves.

This consciousness with which animals are endowed is limited and is restricted to what is only within the scope of their individuality, never without referring to a sense of recognition of their own gender, this type of consciousness deserves to be called nothing other than instinct.

> (...) Consciousness in the sense of a sense of self, the capacity for sensory discernment, perception and even judgment of external things according to certain sensory characteristics, this kind of consciousness cannot be denied to animals.[34]

In this way, man's main difference from animals lies precisely in consciousness in its strictest sense, which allows him to go beyond himself and recognize his own gender. Because they are unable to go beyond their own individuality and have their own gender as an object of knowledge, animals have a limited consciousness. However, this limitation of the animal's consciousness does not mean that they are in an inferior situation to man. Proof of this can be found in *The Essence of Christianity* (1841), where Feuerbach uses a simple caterpillar as an example. The limitation of an animal's consciousness, like the caterpillar, refers in the same way to the limitation of its own life and consequently there is no need to go beyond what is essential (necessary) for itself. Feuerbach means that if the consciousness of any animal satisfies its needs, then this consciousness has reached its highest degree of perfection and there is no demand for anything beyond its own essence.

Religion, according to Feuerbach, is nothing more than the generic essence of man externalized, so religion, as the objectification of the essence of a being, can only be established for those who recognize their own gender: man. We can thus base ourselves on the sentence in which the author states, in an apparently simple way, that the essential difference between man and animal is: *Animals have no religion* (FEUERBACH, 1988), precisely because they have no gender consciousness. This first

---

[34] FEUERBACH. Ludwig. [1841]. *The Essence of Christianity*. Trad. By Jose da Silva Brandao. Papirus editora. 1988, p. 48.

statement, although seemingly quite simple, actually masks something quite complex: the perfection of consciousness.

Consciousness is revealed in man by the fact that he knows that he knows, that is, the thought that can think itself countless times. The very classification of the species *homo sapiens sapiens*, meaning the man who knows that he knows, refers to this quality of the person who possesses consciousness. After all, the etymology of the word itself comes from *conscientia*, which in turn comes from *scire*, meaning to *know,* and consequently, if consciousness is aware of itself, then it necessarily becomes the object of knowledge of itself, thus revealing its character of infinitude and perfection. Infinitude because it can analyze itself infinitely many times and perfection because it is satisfied with itself and needs nothing more.

> Consciousness is the hallmark of a perfect being; consciousness exists only in a satisfied, complete being. Human vanity itself confirms this truth. Man looks at himself in the mirror; he is pleased with his figure. This pleasure is a necessary, spontaneous consequence of perfection, of the beauty of his image .[35]

The perfection of consciousness is something of total relevance for us to understand God, since the perfection of God as an infinite and complete being can only be understood by what is also infinite and complete, that is, perfect. Although it is trapped in a sensitive, finite and imperfect body, human consciousness only reaches the idea of infinity because it is itself infinite and religion is nothing more than man's awareness of infinity.

> Consciousness is essentially of a universal, infinite nature. The consciousness of the infinite is nothing other than the consciousness of the infinitude of consciousness. Or again: in the consciousness of the infinite, the finitude of its own essence is an object for the conscious .[37]

Feuerbach's aim in describing consciousness in its most intimate,

---

[35] FEUERBACH. Ludwig. [1841]. *The Essence of Christianity.* Trad. By Jose da Silva Brandao. Papirus editora. 1988, p. 48.

essential sense is, in fact, to describe the essence of man. However, this is only possible, according to the philosopher, by using elements that are external to man himself to explain what is internal to him, i.e. his essence can only be known, revealed, through objects, never directly, i.e. through himself.

> Man is nothing without objects. Great men, exemplary men, who reveal to us the essence of man, confirmed this phrase with their lives. They had only one dominant fundamental passion: the
> achievement of the goal that was the fundamental object of their activity.[38]

2.3 Objective Theory

In Feuerbachian philosophy, objects are of great importance, whether material or spiritual, because they serve as an intermediary for man to become aware of what is most intimate to him. Sensory or spiritual objects are the means by which man gains access to his essence.

Man's essence is first externalized so that he can then find it within himself. When the objects through which man identifies his essence are material, i.e. sensory, these objects have a difference from man, which makes them easily identifiable and discernible. But when the objects are spiritual or religious, then it is extremely difficult to disassociate them from man, because these objects are in man's own consciousness.

In the sensory object, man can easily be separated from it, since this type of object is outside of him. In the case of spiritual or religious objects, it is more difficult to separate them from man, because man's awareness of himself is what gives rise to the object itself, in which he externalizes his essence. It is necessary to reinforce the idea that man's awareness of himself is what gives rise to the religious object, yet this awareness is not recognized by him as something projected onto the external object, i.e. God, and that it returns to himself as something alien to him.

The essence of man is what is most intimate to him and can

therefore only be known if it is revealed externally through objects. In Feuerbach's philosophy, man's relationship with nature is always present, because it is through this relationship between man and nature and, consequently, with objects, whether material or spiritual, that his innermost secrets can truly be known.

> The object to which the subject is essentially and necessarily related is nothing other than this subject's own, objective essence. If this is an object common to many individuals who are different in species but the same in kind, then it is, at least in the way in which it is an object for these individuals according to their difference, a proper but objective being .[36]

The aforementioned passage is intended to demonstrate how the objectified essence of a being is projected onto an object, which is a necessary and obligatory element for this essence to be known, i.e. from the relationship between a being and the object, the relationship between this being and itself is found. Objects, in fact, are a mirror through which the essence of a being is projected and reflected back to itself so that in this way man has contact, albeit indirect, with what he really is. Feuerbach uses the relationship between the Earth and the Sun as an example in his book *The Essence of Christianity*.

> The sun is the common object of the planets, but just as it is an object for Mercury, Venus, Saturn or Uranus, it is not for the Earth. As a planet, it has its own sun. The sun that illuminates and heats Uranus has no physical (only astronomical and scientific) existence for the Earth; and the sun not only appears differently, it is also really a different sun on Uranus from the one on Earth. [37]

In this example, Feuerbach places the object that is common to other beings as the object through which all of them, the planets, reveal their essence, yet the essence of each planet is not the same, and this difference is known precisely because of the relationship that each planet, with its distinct essence, has with the object, although it is the same in common, it is not the same for each planet because of its relationship with each of those

---

[36] FEUERBACH. Ludwig. [1841]. *The Essence of Christianity*. Trad. By Jose da Silva Brandao. Papirus editora. 1988, p. 49.
[37] Ibidem, p. 44.

who reveal their essence by having it as their object. The Sun that bathes the Earth is not the same as the one that hits the surface of Uranus, but the relationship between the Sun and the Earth is not the determining factor for the Earth, whose essence is only known through the Sun.

> This is why the relationship between the Earth and the sun is at the same time a relationship between the Earth and itself or its own essence, because the proportion of the magnitude and intensity of the light with which the sun is an object for the Earth is the proportion of the distance that determines the Earth's own nature. Every planet therefore has in its sun the mirror of its own essence .[38]

So we can conclude that the relationship between the being and the object consists concomitantly in the relationship between the being and itself, and it is precisely because of the existence of the object that this relationship becomes possible. The awareness we have of what is external to us and allows us to know something that is internal, intimate, is the same as the awareness we have of ourselves.

The essence that is revealed through the object is in itself perfect. Feuerbach bases this perfection not for nothing, but because it is the foundation of itself. What is the essence of man? Will, reason and heart. Why does the author refer to them as something perfect? Only because they have their purpose in themselves. But if they are purposes in themselves, then wouldn't the existence of objects be dispensable in order to reveal them? Objects are exactly what make it possible for the essence of man to be known, that is, as if they were a mirror for the human essence itself, which, once projected, can turn towards man himself and thus be known.

For Feuerbach, man is nothing without objects, because his essence is not directly aware of itself. In order for man to know his essence, he must have contact with that which allows him to reach everything that is most intimate and inner only through what is external to him, the objects.

---

[38] Ibidem, p. 46.

Feuerbach wants to say that the object of religion, precisely because it is an object found in the individual himself, is intertwined with him in such a way that it becomes practically impossible to distinguish it from man without the use of critical judgment.

> The sensory object is in itself an indifferent object, independent of intention, of judgment; but the object of religion is a more selected object: the most excellent being, the first, the highest; it essentially presupposes a critical judgment to distinguish between the divine and the non-divine, the adorable and the non-adorable .[39]

Because it is found in man's own awareness of himself, the religious object expresses, like no other, what is deepest in man. God is the object of religion, and so, as a symbol, he represents man's thoughts, intentions, values and his own knowledge of himself and what he wants to achieve one day, and when we separate God from man, we separate man from himself.

> However man thinks, however he intends, so is his God: how much value man has, how much value and no more does his God have. *The consciousness of God is man's consciousness of himself, the knowledge of God is man's knowledge of himself.* Through God you know man and vice versa through man you know his God; both are the same thing .[40]

Feuerbach makes it clear that religious man has no direct awareness of himself as a religious being. As has already been said, man has no direct knowledge of his essence, except through objects. This fact reveals itself as the first aspect that is fundamental to the existence of religion. It is precisely the fact that man does not know that what is most intimate and essential to him is being projected onto something that he considers to be totally alien, different and diverse from himself that makes the existence of religion possible in a very peculiar way.

> [...] It should not be understood here as if the religious man were directly aware of himself, that his awareness of God is the awareness he has of his own essence, because the lack of awareness of this fact is what underlies the peculiar essence

---

[39] FEUERBACH. Ludwig. [1841]. *The Essence of Christianity.* Trad. By Jose da Silva Brandao. Papirus editora. 1988, p. 46.
[40] FEUERBACH. Ludwig. [1841]. *The Essence of Christianity.* Trad. By Jose da Silva Brandao. Papirus editora. 1988, p. 55.

of religion.[41]

The peculiar essence of religion lies precisely in this fact. Man cannot find himself as man in the object of worship, which seems to be absolutely alien to him. For him, the awareness he has of God is the awareness of another being. It is due to this fact that religion establishes itself as the first knowledge that man has of himself, albeit indirectly, preceding even philosophy. The being that expresses all that he is and presupposes him is not recognized by him as something coming from himself. God only establishes himself as something external to man because man does not perceive in God his own essence, everything that he is and that grounds him as a genus. The awareness we have of religion is the awareness of something alien to man, but which arises from outside man, as something that takes hold of him intimately.

Feuerbach finds in religion the infantile essence of man because it is the first awareness he has of himself and the world around him without realizing that the essence of this divine consciousness is to be found in himself. "Religion is the childish essence of humanity; but the child sees its essence, the human being outside itself - as a child and the object man is to himself as another man." (Feuerbach. 1988).

This means that the two beings, father and son, share the same origin, the latter being responsible for the existence of the former and not the other way around. By not recognizing his essence as something objectified, man sees it as the essence of another being far removed from him. With each new religion, everything that was seen as an object distant from man ends up becoming something that is ever closer to his inner self, or even subjective, making the essence of an alien and diverse being an ever more similar and profound essence, but which is actually his own essence that returns to himself through a spiritual object. Therefore, it can be concluded that the human consciousness that we have of God is nothing

---

[41] Ibidem, p. 52.

more than a consciousness that man has of himself, albeit indirectly, and which can only be known through this religious or spiritual object that is God himself.

CHAPTER 3: SUBJECTIVE FOUNDATION OF RELIGION

In this third chapter, we try to explain Feuerbach's psychological perspective in his lectures of 1851 through the first two subchapters so that, in the last subchapter, the real primary foundation of religion is exposed, the fundamental principle of religion in Feuerbach. Subchapter *3.1 The Feeling of Dependence and Fear* is essential for the psychological foundation of religion, because in man's feeling of dependence on nature lies the primary explanation that gives rise to man's belief in divine beings.
manifestation of fear. In subchapter *3.2 Egoism,* the reason why man feels dependent on something is explained, because it is due to egoism, which Feuerbach clarifies as egoism in the sense of self-preservation, that man begins to worship everything that brings him good, because he loves himself and consequently loves everything that allows him to live. Finally, in the last subchapter, we reconcile the philosopher's two perspectives on religion and its primary foundation.

3.1 The Feeling of Dependence and Fear

Man's relationship with nature is the most important element in explaining religion from a subjective or psychological perspective. For Feuerbach, it is in this relationship that religious sentiment originates, because everything in man's life is first related to nature. Nature is then responsible for imprinting in man everything that makes possible the manifestation of the first signs of religiosity and, consequently, from religion arise the first forms of explanation for all observable and hitherto inexplicable phenomena, which is why the philosopher places religion as the first form of culture or childhood of humanity.

In this sense, the feeling of dependence is fundamental to the existence of religion itself, because without feeling dependent on anything, man would never worship that which is of no importance to him. Feuerbach points out that there is no feeling of dependence as a general concept, but rather specific and special feelings, such as the feeling of hunger, malaise, sadness in dark times and, above all, the fear of death, which expresses human finitude and everything that arises in its relationship with nature.

For Feuerbach, the feeling of finitude in relation to life is the most delicate for man, because this feeling expresses nothing more than the awareness that one day he will cease to exist, that he will die. This is the greatest of his fears and also what makes, according to the philosopher, man's grave the birthplace of the gods, in other words, there is a direct and inevitable connection between death and religion.

Man is mortal, he doesn't want to die, yet God is immortal, if man were immortal there would be no religion, because the feeling of finitude or dependence, which for the philosopher are the same[42], wouldn't exist either, after all, what would he depend on to exist? What would it be dependent on? The greatest expression of the feeling of finitude or dependence lies in the fact that, for Feuerbach, religion was already innate to man, a bold and powerful statement that deserves some attention to avoid any misunderstanding. In stating that religion is innate, Feuerbach is not referring to the fact that man necessarily manifests belief in some kind of god or even in the sense of the most diverse religions that exist. It is not innate theology, much less a need to believe in a god that is necessary for man's life, but religion as an expression of the feeling of dependence and finitude.

> (...) Religion is essential or innate to man; not religion in the sense of theology or deism, of belief in God itself, but religion as nothing more than man's feeling of finitude and dependence on nature.[43]

It is because of this feeling, or "these", that he worships, respects and even fears his various gods. "The feeling of dependence is the basis of

---

[42] Feuerbach states that religion is the characteristic or quality of a being that necessarily relates to another being, but no god or self-sufficient being is infinite; on the contrary, it is the relationship of dependence between man and nature that expresses the feeling of finitude, so it can safely be said that the two feelings are in fact the same, or to distinguish between them would even be an understatement.

[43] FEUERBACH. Ludwig. [1851]. *Lectures on the Essence of Religion.* Trad. By Jose da Silva Brandao. Papirus editora. 1989, p. 37.

religion, but the primitive object of this feeling is nature, so nature is the first object of religion" (FEUERBACH, 1989, p.29).

In the feeling of dependence, man feels subordinate to the object on which his life depends. From then on, he begins to worship it and even fear it. Fear is one of the most obvious aspects of the feeling of dependence.

> Ancient atheists and even many deists, both ancient and recent, have declared that fear, which is nothing more than the most popular and obvious aspect of the feeling of dependence, is the mainspring of religion .[44]

Feuerbach confirms through his historical examples that fear is an element that is always present in the objects of religious worship. The history of the most primitive peoples proves that most of the gods worshipped were responsible not for the good things in the world, but for the greatest calamities. Evil spirits were worshipped the more cruel they were, but the cult of these evil spirits arises not because their worshippers worship evil or want evil for themselves, on the contrary, evil deities are feared and therefore worshipped because man does not want any harm to come to him and in the hope that the evil spirit will not harm him he makes sacrifices in its name.

> (...) in India there are regions "where most of the inhabitants worship only evil spirits... each of these evil spirits has its own special name and enjoys a worship all the more exquisite the more it is considered cruel and powerful" (Stuhr, *The Religious Systems of the Paid Peoples of the East*). Likewise the American ragas, even those who know of a "supreme being", according to deist reports, worship only the "evil spirits" or the beings to whom they attribute all the evils, illnesses and pains that affect them in order to placate them with this worship, hence out of fear .[45]

This situation of worshipping evil spirits reveals a peculiar characteristic of this type of belief: according to the philosopher, if man is less affected by good than by evil, if he happens to be too naïve to give little

---

[44] FEUERBACH. Ludwig. [1851]. *Lectures on the Essence of Religion*. Trad. By Jose da Silva Brandao. Papirus editora. 1989, p. 30.

[45] Ibidem, p. 31.

importance to the good side of life, then he will worship evil gods, believing them to be more powerful. If the idea or feeling of evil balances out with the idea or feeling of good, then there will be good and bad gods. Finally, if the idea and feeling of good prevails over the idea or feeling of evil, then he will have good gods who will be superior to the evil ones.

In most of the cultures[46] analyzed by the philosopher in his lectures, fear arises from the feeling of dependence and is shown to be a primitive feeling in relation to what man is dependent on. It can be said that this feeling, which the philosopher refers to as the mainspring of religion, is undoubtedly the first to imprint religious sentiment on man. All, or at least most, of nature's most terrifying phenomena are worshipped.

> The rougher peoples, for example, in Africa, North Asia and America fear (as Meiners tells us in his General History and Criticism of Religions according to travelogues) rivers, especially in places where they form dangerous eddies or falls. When they pass such places, they beg for forgiveness or beat their breasts or offer sacrifices to the wrathful deity.[47]

However, it can be understood that fear is only present in these rougher cultures, only among those who still remain in the roughest contact with nature, but Feuerbach clarifies that even in higher cultures such as the Greeks, the cult of the most terrifying phenomena can be found. Among the genius Greeks there was worship of the most terrifying forms of nature, such as Zeus, the god of storm and thunder, the superior being in relation to all the other gods. More generally, what the philosopher means is that the fear of something bad happening to him is what makes man idolize, worship and even make sacrifices so that the angry deity doesn't punish him.

When talking about fear as a fundamental element in the feeling of dependence and, consequently, in religion, we must pay attention not only

---

[46] The cultures that Feuerbach analyzes in his *Lectures on the Essence of Religion* are the redschang inhabitants of the Sumatra region, the Hottentots, the Indians, the Romans when they worshipped diseases, plagues, fevers and promoted festivals with the death of children under the name of Orbona (disgrace).

[47] FEUERBACH. Ludwig. [1851]. *Lectures on the Essence of Religion*. Trad. By Jose da Silva Brandao. Papirus editora. 1989, p. 30.

to that fleeting fear that ends when the storm passes, but rather to fear that is not restricted to a particular object. When mortal danger is imminent, fear is the most obvious and necessary aspect of human life, but as soon as it passes, fear remains. The feeling of being exposed to the hardships of nature remains, if only in the imagination, due to the fact that it could one day happen again.

The explanation of religion based on fear is appropriate, but it is not the only one that exists for religion. In the relationship between man and nature, fear is only the first feeling that arises, because once it is overcome it is followed by an opposite feeling. This feeling is one of gratitude, joy, rapture, which manifests itself at the end of the danger that has gone. Feuerbach ironically points out that, more often than not, the most terrifying and devastating phenomena are those that bring good consequences: "The god who destroys trees, animals and men with his lightning is the same god who revives fields and meadows with his rain. Where evil comes from, there also comes good; where fear comes from, there also comes joy" (FEUERBACH, Ludwig. 1989, p. 33).

We can therefore conclude that the feeling of dependence is the most appropriate psychological explanation for religion and has its beginnings in the relationship that is established between man and nature and nothing else. Feuerbach places man in his rightful place, that is, in nature. According to him, to take nature away from man and place him as a supernatural being is to take away his very essence. For Feuerbach, it is only nature that man depends on to exist and without it he would be nothing, and it is precisely this fact that provides all the elements responsible for religion. Fear exists because nature is the only being that can annihilate human existence at any moment and gratitude arises when the means or causes for being alive remain.

> In short, whoever gives man the means or causes of joy in life will be loved by him, and whoever takes these means from him

or has the power to take them will be feared by him. But both are united in the object of religion: the same thing that is a source of life is also negatively, when I don't have it, a source of death.[51]

3.2 Egoism

For it to be possible for man to feel dependent on something, it is necessary for him to have love for himself; he must first of all have love for himself so that he can then love or worship that which allows him to exist. In this sense, Feuerbach finds in egoism a strong element for religion to be possible.

[51] FEUERBACH. Ludwig. [1851]. *Lectures on the Essence of Religion.* Trad. By Jose da Silva Brandao. Papirus editora. 1989, p. 34.

It's worth noting that the egoism to which the author refers is not egoism in the vulgar sense or an exacerbation of the ego, but, as previously mentioned, a love that man has for himself and that is fundamental to his existence. The sense of the word "egoism" that Feuerbach uses to describe this necessary characteristic for religion does not refer to man's egoism towards man, moral egoism, in which the individual turns his action, even if it is apparently directed towards others, into an action aimed solely at his own advantage, but a natural egoism that is largely responsible for his self-affirmation.

> I understand egoism to mean asserting oneself in accordance with nature and, consequently (because man's reason is nothing other than man's conscious nature) in accordance with reason, man's asserting himself in the face of all the unnatural and anti-human instances that theological hypocrisy, religious and speculative fantasy, brutality and political despotism impose on man. I understand egoism to be the necessary, indispensable egoism, which, as has been said, is not moral but metaphysical, that is, founded on the essence of man without his knowing and wanting, the egoism without which man cannot live; because in order to live I must constantly appropriate what is convenient for me and avoid what is harmful and damaging to me, egoism, because it is in the organism, in the possession of assimilable material and in the refusal of what is not assimilable. By egoism I mean man's love for himself, that is, love for the human essence, the love

> that is the impulse for the satisfaction and improvement of all desires and talents (...) [48]

In dealing with egoism as self-love, Feuerbach also sees the love that the individual feels for others as an indirect love for himself, because man can only love what corresponds to his ideal, his feeling and therefore his essence. This can be seen in the most diverse religions; after all, man only loves what makes sense to him and what is closest to him.

Even in the worship of animals, man doesn't deny himself in any way. By worshipping any kind of religious object, he worships himself, his essence. If he worships dogs, cats or cows, it's because these religious objects somehow represent a good in his life. Or if he worships fleas, lice, worms or any other creature that is insignificant to worship, man only praises it because he believes that this creature will somehow bring him some kind of good, even if such a thought is established only on the basis of imagination. Feuerbach analyzes the relationship that exists in anthropozoomorphism where there is idolatry of the most unusual animals as a moment when man once again worships everything that is fundamental to him or at the very least brings benefits to his existence and consequently feels dependent on it because he values his life. This fact is precisely made possible by egoism, which is an extremely necessary element in religion.

> (...) Man worships as God everything on which he knows or believes that his life depends, and precisely because of this, the object of worship only shows the value he attaches to his life and to himself in general and that, consequently, the worship of God depends on the worship of man .[49]

So we can better understand religion from egoism precisely because egoism is self-love and the self-love that exists in the individual is a fundamental principle for religion. How can man praise and exalt the

---

[48] FEUERBACH. Ludwig. [1851]. *Lectures on the Essence of Religion*. Trad. By Jose da Silva Brandao. Papirus editora. 1989, p. 50.
[49] FEUERBACH. Ludwig. [1851]. *Lectures on the Essence of Religion*. Trad. By Jose da Silva Brandao. Papirus editora. 1989, p. 50.

divinities if he despises himself? Can he worship a being who brings him good if he doesn't want good for himself? For man to recognize and praise an objectively supreme being, he must have it subjectively within himself. In contrast to this, Feuerbach uses the example of the suicidal person who repudiates and despises life. In this case, man is in a state of disgrace or pathology, not in the normal state of life, because his life lacks the qualities and goods that are part of normal life, and so he no longer has life.

> The suicidal person does not take his own life; it has already been taken from him. That's why he kills himself; he only destroys an illusion; he only throws away a shell whose core, whether it's his fault or not, has long since rotted away. But in the normal state of health and when the concept of life is understood to mean the content of all man's essential goods, life is quite rightly the most precious good, the highest essence of man.[50]

In the end, Feuerbach comes to the conclusion that man is dependent on egoism for everything that is important for his existence, everything that he wants and needs. Egoism is the starting point for the existence of the need that makes man dependent on everything that brings good to his life. He only divinizes the elements responsible for his existence because for him his life is something extremely divine, in other words, man only worships the gods who bring him good in some way, because self-love, which is egoism, gives rise to man's feeling of dependence on nature.

3.3 The Anthropological and Subjective Foundations of Religion

So far, the arguments by which Feuerbach bases religion from his different points of view have been exposed, that is, religion has been explained in its anthropological aspect, emphasizing the perfection of the human race, and its psychological or subjective aspect, in which the importance of nature for the existence of religion has been demonstrated. In the latter, man is treated as an almost null being, depreciated in his

---

[50] FEUERBACH. Ludwig. [1851]. *Lectures on the Essence of Religion.* Trad. By Jose da Silva Brandao. Papirus editora. 1989, p. 52.

relationship with nature, which does not correspond to his desires and therefore personifies him, giving rise to the figure of gods whom he then worships.

This research began with Feuerbach's description of man and the difference between his narrow individual sense and his broad generic sense, because from this conceptualization it becomes clear why Feuerbach treats the human race as something perfect and therefore God. Therefore, in the difference between the individual and the genus lies the difference between perfection and nullity. The man described in *The Essence of Christianity* is almost a counterpoint to the one Feuerbach describes in his lectures of 1851, since, from the subjective aspect of religion, all human nullity, finitude and imperfection can be seen.

Religion arises in the life of man precisely because he is the bearer of consciousness in its strictest sense. Man manages to have his own gender for himself, through this ability he manages to have the I and the Thou for himself and from then on he has a double life, as described in the first chapter. For the religious phenomenon, Feuerbach adds that because they share the same essence, man and God are the same being. However, it is worth remembering, as stated above, that the man he is referring to is not man in the strict individual sense, but man in his broad generic sense, man as a genus.

Therefore, the human essence based on will, reason and heart are perfections because they have their purpose in themselves and cause all the perfection of the genre to be externalized and objectified. In this sense, Feuerbach makes it clear that the objects in man's life are the only means by which he can have contact or even knowledge of his own essence, because human consciousness has no direct contact with its essence.

God himself is a spiritual object that brings to man's knowledge what he most longs for, desires, wants for himself, and thus becomes a public confession of his innermost secrets. However, when we speak of God, we necessarily speak of man, because the two share the same essence, so God and man are one and the same! It is more difficult to distinguish between God and man simply because they share the same consciousness, since, unlike sensory objects, God is in man and intimate to him. For Feuerbach, man is the God of man, although he doesn't realize it, because he alienates his own essence outside of himself and when it returns to him, it returns as another essence.

The generic essence of man is the foundation of religion. But this foundation is only made possible through material, empirical means, present in the very objects that are part of human life, which are established through their relationship with nature. Man is the bearer of an essence, but this essence can only be known once it has been objectified and externalized through material means.

In order for its essence to be objectified, transformed into an object of knowledge, there is a need for a sensible, material relationship with the only thing that presupposes it, that is, nature. From this point on we enter into what is the philosopher's main object of study in his lectures, the non-reciprocal relationship between man and nature.

In the exposition that follows throughout the lectures of 1851, Feuerbach changes his focus on what underlies religion, but at no point does he seek another justification for the fundamental principle of religion, much less contradict himself. What ends up happening is that the perspective on the same subject is divergent, but the primary explanation behind it is the same.

In the relationship between man and nature, the feeling of dependence and egoism exist because man has a consciousness of himself and also a consciousness of gender, which is responsible for the objectification of all human capacities, in fact their generic essence in God.

However, throughout his texts, the author never establishes a hierarchy in relation to his different points of view on what underlies religion. There is no primary explanation for the religious phenomenon, i.e. religion does not arise primarily because of the perfection of the human essence or the feeling of dependence, but rather because these are the most important and therefore necessary elements for the existence of religion. However, none of them appears to be more or less important than the others. This ultimately leads Feuerbach's arguments to the same conclusion, that is, religion is based on the arguments presented in the two works, because they are equivalent. Religion is the living room of a house and what Feuerbach does in the two works is look at it through two different windows, opposite each other, in other words, the philosopher's object of study is only presented to us through different prisms revealing the same underlying cause.

FINAL CONSIDERATIONS

In this work we can see the importance that Feuerbach attached to this delicate subject of religion. Even today, we can see that it is not easy to deal with something so subjective, profound and which provokes the most controversial emotions in people. What Feuerbach proposed throughout his works, in fact, was not simply to destroy God, because to destroy God is to destroy man himself, after all they are the same being, they share the same essence. On the contrary, the philosopher proposed a new ethic based on man's relationship with himself without the intermediary of divinities, an affirmation of man based on the negation of God.

The divergence between the two works is quite obvious, which is why it was necessary to investigate what the philosopher considered to be the fundamental principle of religion. It could not be said with certainty that religion is founded on a single element or on several without a thorough and complete investigation of his two main works. In this way, it proved to be very relevant and opportune to articulate the main concepts of Feuerbach's philosophy, such as the perfection of the human race, consciousness, the theory of objectification, the feeling of dependence and egoism, in order to find that first foundation which is truly responsible for engraving in man the belief in his most diverse gods.

In the first chapter, all the problems that exist in Feuerbach's vision in the two works were exposed in order to clearly and distinctly consolidate the fact that this divergent vision exists and needs to be clarified. The second chapter showed that Feuerbach distinguishes between man in the general sense and man in the individual sense, with the former being responsible for all divine perfection, since the human essence is concentrated in him, which for the philosopher is perfect and ends up manifesting itself through objects, as discussed in the following subchapter.

As we enter the third chapter, we notice that the elements responsible for religion are different. The essences that were set out in the previous chapter and which represented all the perfection of the human race have given way to the necessary, and also the only existing, relationship between man and nature, in order to establish the assumptions responsible for the origin of religion. The feeling of dependence and egoism were shown to be key elements in understanding the psychological causes engraved by nature in man and which generated the first and most rudimentary forms of worship of the most diverse aspects of nature. Feuerbach explains why nature had been left out of his previous work, *The Essence of Christianity*. According to him, Christianity is the religion of morality and not of nature, and he proposes a religion of man with what really presupposes him, not God, but nature itself. However, at no point does Feuerbach try to divinize it or even worship it, the philosopher simply puts it in its proper place without the exaggerations characteristic of religion.

Finally, still in the third chapter, more precisely in the last sub-chapter, a conclusion was made that clarifies the fundamental principle responsible for religion. To this end, the causes of religion, both psychological and anthropological, are equivalent to the same foundation. Religion does not originate solely because of the mishaps that have arisen in the life of man in his non-reciprocal relationship with nature. It's not just the feeling of dependence or finitude, or even man's awareness that one day he will cease to exist, that he will die. But all of these elements make man alienate his essence from himself, and see it as something that is not part of himself, but rather as something that exists by itself and in itself, independent of him.

Throughout his works, Feuerbach showed a great concern for man. For him, man must replace love for God with love for others as a single religion, leaving faith in God for man's faith in himself; by denying God, man affirms himself. Man must have faith in himself and not in an external being superior to him. From himself he will swallow his own destiny in which man's only demon is the rude, superstitious, selfish and cruel man who must be avoided.

REFERENCES

MAIN BIBLIOGRAPHY

FEUERBACH, Ludwig. *The Essence of Christianity.* Campina- SP: Papirus, 1988.

Lectures on the Essence of Religion.
Campina-SP: Papirus, 1989.

COMPLEMENTARY BIBLIOGRAPHY

REDYSON, Deyve. CHAGAS, Eduardo F. *Ludwig Feuerbach: Philosophy, Religion and Nature.* Sao Leopoldo, RS: Nova Harmonia, 2011.

SERRAO, Adriana Verissimo. *The Humanity of Reason - Ludwig Feuerbach and the Project of an Integral Anthropology.* Lisbon: Calouste Gulbenkian Foundation, 1999.

SOUZA, Draiton Gonzaga. *Feuerbach's Anthropological Atheism.* Porto Alegre-RS: EDIPUCRS, 1994.

SERRAO, Adriana Verissimo. *The Humanity of Reason - Ludwig Feuerbach and the Project of an Integral Anthropology.* Lisbon: Calouste Gulbenkian Foundation, 2005.

SECONDARY BIBLIOGRAPHY

GIMENES DE PAULA, Marcio. *The Future of an Illusion: Some Reflections between Feuerbach and Freud.* In: www.psicanaliseefilosofia.com.br/adverbum/.../feuerbach

SARTORIO, Lucia Aparecida Valadares. *Feuerbach's Anthropology - and Some Delineations About a Possible Influence on Marx's Thought.* In:
www.verinotio.org/di/di15_antropologia.pdf

SEMINERIO, Franco Lo PrestL **Religion as a Psychological Process.**
Temas em Psicologia - 1998, Vol. 06 N° 02.In:
http://**pepsic.bvsalud.org/pdf/tp/v6n2/v6n2a09.pdf.** 1999.

More Books!

I want morebooks!

Buy your books fast and straightforward online - at one of world's fastest growing online book stores! Environmentally sound due to Print-on-Demand technologies.

Buy your books online at
www.morebooks.shop

Kaufen Sie Ihre Bücher schnell und unkompliziert online – auf einer der am schnellsten wachsenden Buchhandelsplattformen weltweit! Dank Print-On-Demand umwelt- und ressourcenschonend produziert.

Bücher schneller online kaufen
www.morebooks.shop

info@omniscriptum.com
www.omniscriptum.com

OMNIScriptum

www.ingramcontent.com/pod-product-compliance
Ingram Content Group UK Ltd.
Pitfield, Milton Keynes, MK11 3LW, UK
UKHW041935131224
452403UK00001B/149